Project Management Skills for Coursework

PROJECT MANAGEMENT SKILLS FOR COURSEWORK

A Practical Guide to Completing
BGCSE Exam Coursework

Dorcas M. T. Cox MBA, PMP

iUniverse LLC
Bloomington

PROJECT MANAGEMENT SKILLS FOR COURSEWORK
A PRACTICAL GUIDE TO COMPLETING
BGCSE EXAM COURSEWORK

iUniverse books may be ordered through booksellers or by contacting:

iUniverse LLC
1663 Liberty Drive
Bloomington, IN 47403
www.iuniverse.com
1-800-Authors (1-800-288-4677)

ISBN: 978-1-4917-0050-1 (sc)
ISBN: 978-1-4917-0051-8 (e)

Printed in the United States of America.

iUniverse rev. date: 11/02/2013

To my mother, Ena-mae T. Cox, Desiree Cox, and David Allens, as well as all others who dare to believe and have the courage to try.

Thank you Kim Bodie, Kmchell Dodge, and Astrid-Adjuah Cleare for your positive contributions in the areas of mentoring and youth empowerment.

TABLE OF CONTENTS

PREFACE

When I began teaching project management certification classes in 2010, I focused on preparing adult learners to sit and successfully pass the Project Management Professional (PMP) exam and the Certified Associate in Project Management Exam (CAPM). These are globally recognized designations awarded by the Project Management Institute.

Astrid Adjuah Cleare, a student in my first cohort, quickly became my friend. My requirements were that students applied the project management processes to real-world projects.

During one Saturday class, Adjuah asked, "What real-world project are you doing, Dorcas? How are you applying project management processes in ways that make a difference?"

Her question stopped me in my track. I began thinking.

Adjuah shared her passion for youth empowerment with me, and I adopted it as my own. Our vision became the Bahamas General Certificate of Secondary Education Examination (BGCSE). The BGCSE is a national examination that culminates in a three-year program intended to equip students with marketable skills upon completion. The examination generally consists of three components, one of which is called the coursework. Coursework is a research project. Coursework is compulsory and is a perfect avenue to apply project management processes to youth audiences and positively impact national test scores in the Bahamas. Others partnered with us. Our vision developed with support from Rochelle Lightbourne, Tanya McCartney, Kim Bodie, Miguel Pratt, Kmchell Dodge, David A. Brown, Antonio Butler Jr., Daniel Bayssassew, Rachael Brown, Jordan Peterson, Gwendolyn Johnson, Cheryl Bowe-Moss, Keyshan Cartwright-Bastian, Ross Smith, Michelle Sears to name a few. Special thank you to The Hon. Jerome Fitzgerald M.P., Minister of Education, Science, and Technology for giving us the opportunity to present this body of work to the business subject teachers.

For two weeks in the summer of 2011, we piloted our material to a group of tenth—and eleventh-grade students at Aquinas College in the Bahamas. These students applied project management processes to the BGCSE coursework requirements. We learned from the school's principal (Mrs. Shona Knowles), subject teachers, and students. We continued working.

As I taught more sessions of my professional classes, read books, and interacted with others, I continued learning and developing techniques for breaking down concepts often described as "quite technical" in easy-to-understand ways that were applicable to everyday life.

My sister said, "Simplifying the concepts broadens the audience appeal."

Adjuah says, "Find ways of teaching people how to apply project management to everyday life."

My teenage son says, "Make it interesting."

It's a tall order.

Each of the four chapters of this book applies project management processes—from analyzing goals and identifying stakeholders to managing expectations, overcoming barriers, communicating effectively, and monitoring and evaluating progress and results.

This compelling saga introduces concepts that may mirror your experiences. In relating to the concepts and becoming engrossed in their application, you may experience elements of your life unfolding.

My teenage son will begin coursework in the upcoming school year. The contents of this book have supported him in successfully completing his requirements.

I have made a difference through the work that I do. This book contributes to that work.

INTRODUCTION

It can be a challenge to analyze information in ways that compares and contrasts, justifies a stand, supports and defends an argument, or creates a new product, outcome, or point of view. Coursework is an avenue to question, test, evaluate, and formulate. It is also an opportunity to innovate.

This book teaches you how to think through concepts and ideas. It shows how to develop greater skills in expecting and addressing change.

Who Should Read This Book?

Project Management Skills for Coursework is intended to captivate the interest of persons who are

- writing BGCSE coursework for various subjects (particularly business subjects);
- conducting and writing research papers;
- new to the field of project management;
- required to execute projects in accordance with a project plan;
- aspiring to roles with increasing responsibilities that include, and are not limited to, project management;
- focusing on real-world, practical applications of project management; and increasing
- breadth and depth of project management knowledge.

How to Read This Book

Project Management Skills for Coursework is written in ways that allow you to cover the book sequentially or skip to chapters that address specific concerns. Chapters contain expert tips that help increase knowledge, skills, and confidence while avoiding mistakes, saving time and money, and increasing productivity.

CHAPTER 1

STARTING THE PROJECT

After studying this chapter, you should be able to

- define coursework;
- define a project;
- differentiate between projects,
- programs, and portfolios;
- list and describe project management skills that may be used to complete the coursework project;
- describe key behaviors that are included as a part of ethics;
- describe the importance of having a project vision;
- define what it means to start a project;
- explain the importance of starting a project;
- describe the importance of a start up checklist;
- and recognize the importance of talking to the right people.

Way before entering eleventh grade, John's life seemingly escapes him. Other than a collector's edition of electronic games and devices, he has nothing much to show. His daily routine hardly involves academic studies—too many disappointments, average grades, and a goal of cracking the 3.0 grade point average mark that he may never achieve. John is broken and ashamed of himself. He's more affected by his previous end-of-year report card than he thought he would be. He knows that he has potential, feeling quite often on the verge of a breakthrough, but with no real plan or direction, drifting is the order of the day.

Looking down the barrel of another school year; he certainly doesn't expect changes in his life, and he can't see anything to be gained by losing sleep over it. It's a safe bet that—as in previous years—John can find lots of ways to take his mind off of school. Looking around in the quiet auditorium, he notices the peeling paint from the ceiling. The remaining window panes are struggling to hold onto the screens for companionship. Outside a security officer affectionately known as Seque awaits unwelcomed visitors.

The deafening applause pulls John from his daytime sleep. In his disorientated state, he tries to pull together thoughts projecting them toward the direction of the podium.

Principal Collie is poised to deliver his charge. "Students, I admonish you to take the BGCSE coursework seriously. Coursework accounts for 30 percent of your overall grade. Take the BGCSE coursework seriously."

John swallows, drawing himself comfortably into a nestled position in his chair. He turns off the lights, relaxing into another daytime snooze.

Although Freddie isn't a fan of Principal Collie, he's famous for a sometimes annoying habit of quoting faculty whenever he wishes to prove a point to his advantage.

"Wasn't it Principal Collie who said to take the BGCSE coursework seriously because it accounts for 30 percent of your overall grade?" he asks with a smirk.

"Freddie, I may as well tell you, I don't really understand what coursework is," John says.

"Seriously? Surely, this can't be classified information," Freddie replies.

"I really don't care what you do with the information. I'm not trying to impress you—or anyone else for that matter. I just need you to help me out. I need a better understanding of BGCSE coursework," John says.

"I'll hold on to the information, if you don't mind, while I help you. Are you sure that you're asking the right person for help?"

Nodding, John says, "Seven As in BJC, editor of the school newspaper, president of the Debating Society, and sitting BGCSE exams in eight subjects this year? Yeah, you're the one," John says.

"Okay, I'll talk to my mother about helping you. If she agrees, we'll catch the bus to my mother's office after school every afternoon starting tomorrow. After she gets off work at 4:30pm, we stay behind for two hours and she tutors me. You have to check with your parents as well to see if it's okay with them. Write down my phone number so your mother can call my mother tonight to discuss it and make the arrangements."

"Thanks."

"No problem, man. I don't mind helping you out. At least you're trying to help yourself. That's more than I can say for some of the others."

In the reception area where Freddie's mother works, the receptionist glances at the boys and shoots them a bright smile, which they return in kind. After a few moments of introductions and exchanging pleasantries, they stroll casually toward Freddie's mother's office. The twosome reach the end of the corridor, stop abruptly in front of a door, knock, and enter when a friendly voice beckons them.

Freddie grins from his left ear to his right at the sight of his mother.

She is his mirror image; the only distinctions are the differences in age and gender.

Freddie's mother introduces herself as Mrs. Davis and informs John about who she is and what she does for a living.

As an icebreaker, John welcomes Mrs. Davis into his life, sharing his passion for music, his electronic game collection, and his career ambition of becoming a lawyer.

With the introductions safely tucked away, they begin discussing the topic of BGCSE coursework that, for John, begins a journey of learning and charting a course toward achieving his career ambition.

Definition and Purpose of Coursework

Freddie's mother explains the purpose of coursework as a way in which students expand their abilities to develop and apply logical and critical thinking skills across many topic areas. She explains how life often presents lots of scenarios from simple to complex, all of which require demonstration of certain behaviors and skills. Some scenarios in life may be solved by just recalling past events. Other scenarios may be resolved through troubleshooting ideas or concepts. Sometimes we must move beyond just understanding to applying information in new ways by interpretation and demonstration. Analyzing information in ways that compare and contrast, justify a stand, support or defend an argument, and create new products, outcomes, or points of view often confronts us as challenges. Coursework is an avenue to question, test, evaluate, and formulate. Indeed, coursework is an opportunity to innovate.

"Mrs. Davis, with all due respect, what you describe sounds like the types of things you do at work. We're talking about BGCSE coursework here; it's not that serious."

"So how does it work, John? You graduate on Friday, get a job on Monday, and automatically think analytically, troubleshoot, and solve problems at work? Do you think that's how it works? I'm sorry to burst your bubble.

"Preparation for the workplace begins in tenth grade. Little by little—in subtle ways that you hardly notice—the educational system in high school prepares you for the workplace, university, and life as an adult. In life, just because someone tells you something, does it mean you should believe it?"

"No."

"So how do you determine whether their position makes sense or not?"

"I guess you get some information by reading up on it or discussing it with other people."

"Okay, conduct research and ask other people because you want to do what?" Mrs. Davis's pitch elevates.

"Because you want to get enough information to make a decision?"

"You're asking me—or you're telling me?"

"I'm telling you, Mrs. Davis," John replies timidly.

"Then answer me with conviction, young man. Yes, I agree, you need to examine the facts, information, or opinions of others. Select a position and support it based on the value of the information presented—and then come up with an opinion or a point of view. This is what coursework does." Mrs. Davis leans forward in her chair with nostrils flared. Her eyes are fixed on the boys, and her voice elevates, clearly demonstrating her excitement and passion about the topic.

"Sometimes the greatest gifts that anyone can offer you appear as commonplace objects. I've heard people say that coursework is nothing more than a research paper; apply the skill and behavior necessary to complete coursework correctly, and you will learn that planning and executing the coursework project is a life-changing experience."

Coursework as a Project

"For some subjects, as a student, you choose a topic based on the content that you have covered up to a certain point in the curriculum. For other subjects, you are given a topic. The conclusion is the same in both instances—you begin with a topic and end with an outcome. Coursework is temporary with a clear start date and a clear finish date. It is intended to produce a unique product, service, or result and is developed in greater detail as the work progresses. Coursework fits into the definition of a project."

"Wait a minute, Mummy," Freddie says. "You say that coursework produces a unique outcome. How could the outcome be unique when all of us are using the same syllabus, the same textbook, and the same instructions from the Ministry of Education? I heard that some people are even using the same topic; what's so unique about that? There's only so much you can write about some topics," Freddie says.

"I take your point. Let's say that you and John choose the same topic, do you really think that you both will approach the same topic from the same angle? Do you think that you will use the same results and investigate the same business in the case of a subject like 'Economics, Commerce, and Office Procedures' where visiting businesses may be required. Do you think you will analyze, evaluate, and conclude in the same ways?"

"No."

"Standard methods are used for structure. Sometimes following standard process steps are required based on the discipline and the models associated with certain disciplines. Just because a standard method and processes are used does not mean you will not produce a unique outcome."

Projects, Programs, and Portfolios

"Some students may be taking more than one BGCSE subject with a coursework component. In that case, it may be better to look at grouping the projects into programs or portfolios for greater efficiency as long as the strategy is the same."

"What do you mean by strategy? You mean focus?" John asks.

"Yes. Let's say your focus for approaching this coursework project is to learn how to write a proper research paper to help you in your future.

"From there, take a look at all BGCSE subjects that you will sit where coursework is a requirement. Apply your focus in all instances. In that way, coursework subjects are linked by the same focus. Are you boys following me?"

Both boys nod their head.

"Coursework should be completed from a time-efficiency standpoint. For example, if you are required to complete coursework for subjects like 'Economics, Commerce, and Office Procedures,' which company or companies will you visit? If you determine that the projects for 'Economics, Commerce, and Office Procedures' are related—and that activities required for completing these projects may be managed in a coordinated way to get benefits not available from managing them individually—then you may consider these three related projects as a program. Program management applies knowledge, skills, tools, and techniques to get benefits and control not available by managing projects individually. Program management focuses on project interdependencies and helps determine the best approach for managing them."

"Mummy, not all of my BGCSE subjects are business subjects. I am doing religious studies, science, and art. What am I supposed to do? I can't manage these projects as a program; they don't appear to be related to me."

"You may need to consider a portfolio approach. Projects or programs in the portfolio may not necessarily be interdependent or directly related just as you describe in the case of your unrelated BGCSE coursework projects. Knowing this in advance helps you to manage your time better.

Project Management Skills for Coursework

John is amazed. It's a surprise to him that people talk to each other in this way—that they crave self-development and are passionate about lifelong learning. What would he have been doing otherwise, playing video games? He never thinks about that now. He decides to spend the night fully conscious and alive, controlling his mind from wandering like a stray animal searching for food at night.

John is alert. He listens to Mrs. Davis explain how some people are more self-aware than others are, and they use this skill to manage their behavior in ways that allow them to demonstrate versatility. These people socialize well, recognizing the strengths and weakness in the behavioral styles demonstrated by the people with whom they interact.

On the other hand, there are those who are unable or unwilling to accommodate, conform, or socialize well with others. They demonstrate underdeveloped communication skills and are often labeled outsiders by the group.

She further explains how project management is a discipline where teamwork and cooperation is highly regarded. Selfish and insolated people stand out. While having a good handle on the knowledge of key processes at the foundation of the project management discipline is important, the key to success in managing any project is communication skills. Managing the successful completion of the BGCSE coursework project is no exception. The project environment is filled with opportunities to nourish, develop, and demonstrate leadership, communication, conflict management, and problem-solving skills. Leadership skill is required to motivate others to provide information, resources, direction, and guidance.

"Leadership skill has no age boundaries; it's not a gift for a chosen few," Mrs. Davis says. "Leadership is a skill that may be developed by anyone."

"Mummy, I have a question about delegating. Our project will be disqualified if someone else does it for us. At the same time, it is simply too much work to prepare for in-class quizzes and exams, complete other assignments, continue to participate in extracurricular activities, put in community hours, and complete BGCSE coursework in several subjects."

"There's a fine line that you must not cross when it comes to delegating. If you delegate too much authority, you risk being disqualified. If you delegate too little, you lose useful advice and counsel—and you fail to develop the skill."

"Give me an example of what you mean when you say that if you fail to delegate too little, you lose useful advice and counsel and fail to develop the skill," John says.

"Imagine you need to make an appointment to meet with a businessperson to gather information for your BGCSE coursework project. You are not in the network that the businessperson operates in; you fear that you will never be able to establish the contact without support. You may delegate the responsibility for establishing the contact to someone who operates in the same network as the businessperson. You may even delegate the responsibility for getting your information-gathering questionnaire in this businessperson's hand. This is where the delegating ends in this scenario. It is your job to have the conversation with the businessperson, meet with them to discuss and elaborate upon the feedback obtained from the questionnaire, analyze the data, and document the process and result. Delegating these responsibilities to others results in disqualification of your project and grave consequences for you. Do you see the difference?"

"Yes. You can delegate to the point of making the connection, but from there, you have to do your own work. You can also delegate someone to proofread your work. But you have to accept editorial recommendations and make the changes; they cannot do this for you."

"You got it."

Ethics and Internal Control for Coursework

John recalls vaguely hearing something or reading something about the importance of applying ethics in coursework completion. He doesn't realize that being responsible includes making decisions for the good of his school as well as the organization that he will investigate as the focus of his BGCSE coursework. Mostly, he only thinks about himself.

Mrs. Davis tells both boys about responsibility and how it means admitting mistakes and being accountable for decisions and the consequences that accompany our actions. John is attentive.

Mrs. Davis says, "When we correctly apply the project management processes to completing our BGCSE coursework, we ensure the integrity of our coursework as satisfying the requirements presented by the Ministry of Education. Seeking and obtaining acceptance of our coursework project is a requirement for project closure."

On some level, John accepts that he represents his school on and off campus, in and out of uniform. He knows that he is responsible for following the rules and regulations that apply to his school as well as the rules and regulations that apply to the organization that is the subject of his coursework. What is news to him is that it is his duty to familiarize himself with these rules to ensure that he is not violating them. He wonders where to access the rules. If he comes across information that is sensitive or confidential while completing his coursework requirements, he must not disclose this information to anyone or use the information out of the context for which it is intended. He didn't think that the company would give him access to confidential information. It hadn't occurred to him that the information he might access while completing the coursework would be considered a covenant of trust with the organization.

Mrs. Davis said, "At all times, demonstrate respect in the way we conduct ourselves and the way we treat others when we listen to their viewpoints. Respecting others involves controlling ourselves and our reactions and managing our emotions so we do not engage in shouting matches or ego competitions with others. All of us see the world through our own experiences."

"Mrs. Davis, have you ever experienced the same situation or event as someone else and had a different impression? This happens to me quite often. People say that I see things in a mixed-up way. How is this possible?"

"Perception is the way we use our senses to observe and interpret the world. It is the starting point for individual behavior. Your experiences are not necessarily someone else's experiences. How you see things may be completely different from another person's view and the reality. It doesn't mean that you are right and they're wrong—and it doesn't mean that you think in a mixed-up way."

"That's comforting to know."

"It is important to understand how you see the world and know that you may be interpreting people's behavior based on how you see things and where you are coming from. Keep this in mind if a misunderstanding occurs or if someone who you are working with while you are completing your coursework project is not responding as expected. The way you see things may not always be reality. It's only your interpretation of reality. Be willing to give and take in ways that broaden your outlook to see things in different ways. This is how you continue to learn and grow."

The Project Vision

"I've defined the purpose of coursework, looked at coursework as a project and discovered ways to group coursework projects into programs and portfolios for greater efficiency. We've discussed the project management skills required for coursework completion and the ethics and behavior that you should demonstrate when representing yourself and your school in competing your coursework project. Now let's talk about the project itself and your vision for the project. What is your vision for your coursework project, John?"

"What do you mean by vision?"

"What is your coursework project outcome supposed to accomplish? What is your motivating force for undertaking the coursework project and seeing it through to completion?"

Mrs. Davis says, "What is your vision of success?"

John lifts his head; his voice escapes his lips, slowly and quietly at first. He says, "I need to get good grades in school because I see myself as a lawyer." He is surprised by his words.

"Picture yourself as a lawyer," Mrs. Davis says. "Present your coursework topic to me. What is the focus of your coursework?"

"Automated record systems."

"What about automated record systems? What position are you taking or defending when it comes to automated records systems? What is your vision? Help me to see your vision, John." Mrs. Davis stands.

John says, "My coursework project looks at how workers do their job faster when they use automated records systems and they like their job. This is my project vision."

It would be days before he would see Mrs. Davis again. He is nervous and uneasy, but he's never been so excited about learning. John is not aware of it, but he operates on another level.

John's inside voice says, "Settle yourself. Write the project start up checklist and the list of people to talk to as an assignment from Mrs. Davis."

Project Start up Checklist

Mrs. Davis asks John to write a project start up checklist to lay out the project start up process for the following reasons. Project start up does the following:

- outlines what you will and will not do, giving you more focus
- helps you to begin thinking about progress markers for your project
- includes input from people who can help
- guides you in thinking about your requirements, initial risks, quality considerations, and what is acceptable

Step 1—Know Your Purpose

State your purpose. For example, my coursework project looks at how workers do their job faster when they use automated records systems and they like their job.

Step 2—Know the Ministry's Purpose

Review the Ministry of Education requirements for the coursework project outlined in the Coursework Guide.

Step 3—Look at the Risks

- May be difficult to find information.
- Some people who I need help from may not support the project.
- May not have enough time to finish all of the work.
- May be challenging to find a business willing to agree to be investigated for the sake of the project.
- Employees may be suspicious and not helpful.
- Not enough people may fill in the survey so there is not information to work with.
- Business may not have enough people to be surveyed who use the automated records management system.
- Business that agrees to be surveyed may not have an automated records management system.
- May be hard to get the surveys out and collect them again.
- Analyzing the data may be time consuming and challenging.
- May not have access to photocopier to print coursework and questionnaires.

Talk to the Right People

John finally concentrates. It's hard to pull away from his chores. He doesn't have much time; he'll have to use it wisely. He works weekends and sometimes after school to earn the money that contributes toward groceries and odds and ends for his family. Things are tough and times are hard in John's home. There is not much support around in terms of attention to John's interest when it comes to his schoolwork either. But that's all right now. He has Mrs. Davis for inspiration—and Freddie as his only friend and mentor.

"Hmm . . ." he says, Mrs. Davis has asked him to complete a list of the people who he needs to talk to. This is important, it really makes you stop and think about who you need on your side working with you to help you to get this coursework done.

John mumbles, "This might take a while, but not that many people even know I'm taking BGCSE coursework. What do they have to gain or lose from my success?"

Before moving on to the next chapter, complete the discussion questions to understand how the information in this chapter may help you.

Key Points to Remember

- Coursework is a way to develop and apply logical and critical thinking skills by using practical research.
- Coursework challenges us to question, test, evaluate, and formulate.
- A project is temporary with a clear start date and clear finish date that produces a unique product, service, or result and is developed in greater detail as the work progresses.
- Programs are groups of related projects managed with the same techniques in a coordinated fashion.
- Managing projects collectively as programs makes it possible to capitalize on benefits that would not be achievable if the projects were managed separately.
- Portfolios are a collection of programs and projects that support goals and objectives.
- Some people are more self-aware than others—and they use this skill to manage their behaviors in ways that allow them to demonstrate versatility. These people socialize well and

recognize the strengths and weakness in the behavior styles demonstrated by the people who they interact with.

- Talk to the right people who are actively involved in your project—and have something to gain or lose from your coursework success or failure.
- Project management is a discipline where teamwork and cooperation are highly regarded.
- The project environment is full of opportunities to develop and demonstrate leadership, communication, conflict-management, and problem-solving skills.
- Leadership skill is required to motivate others to provide information, resources, direction, and guidance.
- There is a fine line that you must not cross when it comes to delegating. If you delegate too much authority, you risk being disqualified. If you delegate too little, you lose useful advice and counsel—and you fail to develop the skill.
- Ethical standards involve demonstrating responsibility and ensuring integrity.
- The project vision is the motivating force in undertaking the project and seeing it through to completion.
- Investing others in a vision creates value.
- The list of people to talk to is the document that is used to identify people and/organizations impacted by your coursework project.
- You should demonstrate strong communication skills at all times when it comes to the coursework project.

Applying to the Next Project

Discussion Questions

1. What is the definition of coursework?
2. What is the definition a project?
3. What is the difference between projects, programs, and portfolios?

4. What are some project management skills that may be used to complete the coursework project?
5. What are ethics?
6. Why are ethics important?
7. What are some key behaviors that are included as a part of ethics?
8. Why is it important to have a project vision?
9. What do you have to do to start a project?
10. What is the importance of a start up checklist?
11. Why is it important to list the right people to talk to?

Debrief Questions

1. What are the key learning points?
2. What information was new to you?
3. What concepts will you apply in the future? When?
4. What challenges do you anticipate that may limit your ability to apply the concepts?
5. What needs to be in place to overcome these challenges?
6. Who would you recommend these concepts to and why?

Activity

The following is an activity that may be completed individually or in a small group to assess your comprehension.

1. Answer the discussion questions.
2. Answer the debrief questions.
3. Use the information presented in the chapter and apply to a coursework project of your own.

CHAPTER 2

PROJECT PLANNING

After studying this chapter, you should be able to

Collecting Requirements

- outline the importance of collecting requirements;
- list and describe ways to collect requirements;

Confirming the Topic, Aim, and Objectives

- define the aim;
- outline what should be included as a part of the aim;
- explain the importance of the aim;
- identify what will happen if there is no aim;
- list some components that make up a strong aim;
- define objectives;
- outline the components of objectives;
- list some sample action verbs that may be included in an objective statement;

Using Data Collection Methodology

- define statistics;
- state the importance of statistics;
- explain why knowledge and skill in basic statistical concepts is necessary for BGCSE coursework completion;
- distinguish between descriptive and inferential statistics;
- outline the four elements of descriptive statistical problems;
- explain what is meant by sampling;

- define the five elements of inferential statistical problems;
- state the definition of a population;
- define a variable;
- discuss the importance of measurement;
- define reliability;
- differentiate between the types of data;
- distinguish between the four different ways that you may obtain data;
- explain what is meant by representative sample;
- describe the most common way to satisfy a representative sample requirement;
- state some things that you may consider when deciding on the question type;
- explain the five question types; provide examples of each of the five question types;
- list and describe do's and don'ts of survey administration;

Creating the Outline

- explain the purpose of an outline;

Estimating How Long it Will Take to Complete Each Task in the Outline

- determine how long it will take to complete each task in the outline;

Creating a Schedule

- schedule time to complete each task in the outline;

Focusing on Quality

- state why quality is important in a project;
- describe the process for determining quality;
- explain what may happen if any steps for assuring quality are missed;
- list and describe some steps that may be followed to ensure quality;

Communicating Effectively

- define a communication plan;
- explain the importance of a communication plan;
- indicate what may happen in the absence of effective communication;

Reducing the Risk

- identify risks that may present themselves in a project;
- discuss the methods that may be used to identify risks in a project; and

Managing The List of People to Talk to

- define what is meant by managing the list of people to talk to.

Collecting Requirements

John joins the debating society. Lunchtime meetings result in minimal disruption in his schedule. He still works after school on the evenings he doesn't visit Mrs. Davis with Freddie. At this point, everything is clear—and everything is possible. John's not afraid to dream. At any time in life, people are capable of doing what they dream of. John confidently discovers his ability to succeed.

Freddie says, "Update me, John, on what you've been doing to really understand what the people who will help you need you to do in order to make it easy for them to work with you."

"I've read the Ministry of Education Coursework Guide for the subjects I'm taking—and I've asked my subject teachers who were on my list of people to talk to, to tell me about some of the ethics and behavior requirements that your mother mentioned the other day."

"Did you write this information down?"

John leafs through his composition book and begins reading.

Freddie says, "What are you doing, John?"

"I'm trying to remember what your mother said. Oh yeah . . . here it is. 'Ask people on the list of people to talk to, to describe what they need to have in place to see the coursework project as a success.' My goal should be to find out and prioritize the wants, needs, and expectations of all of the people or organizations that need to support me in completing this coursework project."

"But what about your family? You don't talk about them. Your mother, your father, your sister, and your brothers they should be on the top of the list of people you need to talk to."

"Why are you telling me this?"

"Because I'm trying to help you."

John says, "You've helped me enough by sharing your mother with me. That's all you need to know about my family. I've written down all requirements in enough detail that I can—or anyone else can for that matter—know what needs to be put in place once the coursework project work begins. So far, I've only used the interview technique, but your mother says there are different techniques to find out information from the people who I need to talk to—interviews, questionnaires, even surveys. Is there a best technique to use?"

"It doesn't matter which technique or combination of techniques you use to find out what people who you need help from require to have in place to make it easy for them to help you.

"Thanks for the tip." John says while taking detailed notes.

Confirming the Topic, Aim, and Objectives

John continues learning new things. Another way of looking at things he's experienced before make old things appear new—like the thinking behind compiling the list of people to talk to. He has never thought to talk with people about his project, asking them to share their thoughts and what they need in place to support successful outcomes. He's not used to thinking about things in a big picture way.

Freddie's silence gets John's full attention.

Freddie says, "Let's talk about your aim John. The aim is the backbone of your coursework. The aim tells your reader about your plan for your coursework and forms the basis for your decision."

"Your aim should be written in a way that names the way you will collect the information that you need (surveys, interviews, published data, etc.) and your method for producing your coursework in a way that meets the Ministry's requirements."

"I didn't know you had to do all of this work to complete the BGCSE coursework. I didn't see all of this in the Ministry of Education BGCSE Coursework Guide, and I don't know about anyone else who is going through all of this. Man, I'm not into all of this work!"

Freddie continues, "You can skip planning if you choose and jump right into doing the work like everyone else—but you'll waste time and get tripped up just like they do. My mummy told me that up to 40 percent of the time you put into a project is spent in planning—and I believe her. We've just started planning, and we have plenty more work left to finish before you can begin executing the coursework project. You better settle your nerves before you blow a gasket. Let me educate you about assumptions before I head out because you're already running me hot and getting on my nerves. Assumptions, for the purpose of project management, are things that you believe to be true. You put yourself through this work in order to write down all assumptions and confirm them, allowing you to put a contingency plan in place."

"What do you mean by contingency plan? What's that?"

"What if you plan for a ride to take you to meet with the owner of the business after school on Monday? You assume that the owner will be in office and available when you get there. You assume that someone is making the photocopies of the surveys that you need the workers to complete. You assume that you can borrow my computer on the day when you need it. You assume that the people who you gave the survey to are actually completing them. When you document these assumptions, you can confirm them. By that, I mean that you can confirm that the people who you need to support you have you factored into their plans. This is why you have to talk to people and give them respect by asking them what they need to have in place to support you before assuming that they are just sitting around waiting on you. Why do you think you wrote down the list of people to talk to just to waste more paper in your composition book?

"When you discuss your needs with the people who will help you, you find out if they are available for you. When you get to making up the schedule, you have the courtesy to discuss your project schedule with them so they have you booked in their calendar. If you find that you need to, you can create a backup plan while in planning instead of wasting time backpedaling during execution."

"I'm gone, man. You are seriously on my nerve. You behave like you're the only one who lives in the world. You look like you don't know how to think and care about other people. I don't know what you're into, but I'm not in the mood for you anymore today. Later." With that, Freddie is gone.

John feels sorry for himself. He's ashamed and wants to cry. Freddie is on point in assessing his behavior. For years, he's been told that he does not focus on the needs of others and does not collaborate well in teams. Someone else is saying what others stomached for years. John feels alone and weeps openly.

Mrs. Davis had explained that project management is a discipline where teamwork and cooperation are highly regarded. Selfish and isolated people easily stand out. He'd promised to live in ways that demonstrated greater concern and appreciation for others.

He tries to comfort himself. *Pull yourself together. Stop feeling desperate. You're just in another new place that you must become familiar with.*

John thinks back to a conversation with Freddie.

Freddie said, "Your aim should contain action verbs and measurable outcomes. Your aim is supposed to achieve results; it should be realistic."

Manage my life like a project—now that's a thought. Why not begin by writing an aim?

John takes out his composition book and writes, "I will build stronger relationships by focusing more on the needs and concerns of others and working with others in teams."

The topic sentence in his aim is "I will build stronger relationships," and the controlling idea is "focusing more on the needs of others and working with others in teams." The topic sentence provides the focus. The controlling idea helps provide understanding. The Ministry of Education's BGCSE Coursework Guide states the requirement for including information on the method.

John uses interview technique to collect data from persons who know him best in investigating this claim. *Focus—this isn't all about me.* Perhaps he can kill two birds with one stone. When he engages the people who he needs to talk to about automated records management systems, he could conduct the discussion to prove the aim of his self-development. *Maybe this is what Mrs. Davis meant when she talked about projects, programs, and portfolios. I guess the combination of the BGCSE coursework and my personal development project combine to create a portfolio.*

He decides that he needs an aim for the BGCSE coursework project: Workers do their job faster when they use automated records management systems and they like their job. Internally published data, surveys, and interview techniques will be used to obtain information in support of this claim.

Once he's stated his aim for his portfolio and the method he will use to achieve it, the next step is to write his objectives. Objectives are tactics that are used to achieve the aim. The objectives must support achieving the aim.

John uses these guidelines:

- Each objective should have a single key result.
- If your intent is to achieve more than one result, you should write more than one objective.
- Each result should contribute to your aim.
- Objectives should be measurable. Remember that they are supposed to achieve your aim.
- Consider available resources (time, accessibility to information, etc.).

- Make sure that your objectives are achievable.
- Your objectives should be realistic.
- Take into consideration the constraints and/or outside influences that may threaten the success of your aim.
- Check your stated time frames as a part of your objectives to make sure they are realistic.
- Consider possible delays and how you will be able to overcome these constraints to meet the deadlines you included as part of your objectives.

There are many action verbs that John may choose to use to begin his objective statement. A number of them are outlined below:

achieve	acquire	administer	advocate	analyze	apply
classify	collect	compose	conduct	ensure	establish
explain	explore	propose	rank	research	review

Using Data-Collection Methodology

Mrs. Davis believes that every project must have a vision. A project vision is the motivating force behind taking on a project and seeing it through to the end. Getting people to buy into a vision creates value.

Mrs. Davis continues to teach John, but she is not physically around.

John is enthusiastic. He's searching for something he believes in and desires. He latches on to the concept of managing his life like a project. He needs input from others who he will talk to and learn about their needs and requirements. They will also be his mirror. He needs their feedback and their input. He needs to collect data.

Statistics deal with collecting, classifying, summarizing, organizing, analyzing, and interpreting numerical data. John learns how to properly present and describe information, draw conclusions about large populations based only on information that he gets from samples, recommend improved processes, and make reliable forecasts. In some cases, he gets data from a larger set of data whose characteristics he wishes to estimate. This selection process is called sampling.

John reads that statistics can be classified in two broad areas: descriptive statistics and inferential statistics. Descriptive statistics use numerical and graphical methods to look for patterns in a data set, summarize the information revealed in a data set, and present that information in a convenient form.

Inferential statistics use sample data to make estimates, decisions, predictions, or other generalizations about a larger set of data. John knows that if he uses the area of descriptive statistics when completing his project, his problem will include

- population or samples of interest;
- one or more variables to be investigated;
- tables, graphs, or numerical summary tools; and identification of patterns in the data.

On the other hand, if he uses the area of inferential statistics when completing his project, his problem will include

- population or sample of interest;
- one or more variables to be investigated;
- a population sample;
- inference about the population based on information contained in the sample; and
- a measure of reliability for the inference.

Statistical methods are particularly useful for John when studying, analyzing, and learning about populations. A population is a set of units (usually people, objects, transactions, or events) that interests him as a part of study. Examples of populations include all registered companies in the Commonwealth of the Bahamas, HIV-positive people, and sales made at the drive-through window at Wendy's Thompson Boulevard location last month. Studying a population requires John's focus on one or more characteristics or properties of the units in the population. These are called characteristics variables.

Let's say John's interested in the variables of age, gender, or the number of years of education of people currently unemployed on the island of New Providence. He knows the name variable comes from the fact that any particular characteristic may vary among the units in a population.

Measurement plays an important supporting role in John's statistical studies. Measurement is the process that may be used to assign numbers to variables of individual population units. Perhaps John measures workforce age by simply asking each worker how old he or she is.

For large populations, a reasonable alternative may be to select and study a subset (or portion) of the units in the population. This is called a sample. Statistical inference is an estimate, prediction, or some other generalization about a population based on information obtained in a sample.

Making inferences is only part of the story; John also needs to determine reliability. Reliability is a measure of how good the inference is. The only way that John may be certain that an inference about a population is correct is to include the entire population in his sample. However, because of resource limitations (i.e. insufficient time and/or money), he cannot work with whole populations. Instead, he bases his inferences on a portion of the population, which he refers to as a sample.

In this instance, John introduces an element of uncertainty into his inferences. Therefore, whenever possible, it is important to determine and report the reliability of each inference. He needs a statement about the degree of uncertainty associated with the statistical inference to use as a measure of reliability.

Flipping through the pages of his statistics book, John learns about the two different types of data—quantitative data and qualitative data.

Quantitative Data

Quantitative data is measured on a naturally occurring numerical scale. Examples could be the BGCSE math test scores of one hundred high school graduates or the number of males convicted of murders each year over a five-year period.

Qualitative Data

Qualitative data cannot be measured on a natural numerical scale. Qualitative data can only be classified into categories. Examples include the political affiliation of two hundred voters or a taste tester's ranking of four brands of apple juice.

John's book explains how we often assign arbitrary numerical values to qualitative data for ease of analysis. However, these assigned numerical values are simply codes. They cannot be meaningfully added, subtracted, multiplied, or divided. For example, we might code the taste test in a rank of apple juices from one (best) to four (worst).

These are simply arbitrarily selected numerical codes for the categories and have no utility beyond that. John completes the practice question below.

Practice Question

Imagine that there is intense competition between Sammy's Chicken and KFC Chicken. As a part of Sammy's Chicken's marketing campaign, one hundred persons who eat fast-food chicken are given a blind taste test. After the brand names are disguised, each customer is asked to state a preference for Sammy's Chicken (Brand A) or KFC (Brand B).

1. Describe the population.
2. Describe the variable of interest.
3. Describe the sample.
4. Describe the inference.

Solution

1. The population of interest is the collection or set of all consumers.
2. The characteristic that Sammy's Chicken wants to measure is the consumer's chicken preference as revealed under the

conditions of the blind taste test; the taste preference of fast-food fried chicken is the variable of interest.

3. The sample of one hundred fast-food chicken consumers selected from the population of all fast-food chicken consumers.

4. The inference of interest is the generalization of the fast-food chicken preferences of one hundred sampled consumers to the population of all fast-food chicken consumers. In particular, the preferences of the consumers in the sample may be used to estimate the percentage of all fast-food chicken consumers who prefer each brand.

Practice Question

Classify the following examples of data as either qualitative or quantitative

	Quantitative	Qualitative
Bacteria count in the water of thirty private swimming pools	✓	
Occupation of two hundred shoppers at a supermarket		✓
Marital status of each person living in Gleniston Gardens		✓
Months between auto maintenance for one hundred used cars at Easy Car Sales and Rentals	✓	

Once John decides on the type of data—quantitative or qualitative—appropriate for the situation under investigation, his next step is to obtain data. Generally, he may obtain data in four different ways:

- data from published source
- data from a designed experiment
- data from a survey data collected from observation

Published Data

Published data is already collected and is presented in a published source. Examples of published data include

- books, newspapers, or journals; reports published from the Department of Labor or other government agencies;
- Central Bank report;
- Bahamas handbook; and
- Government of the Bahamas official website.

Designed Experiment

Since Freddie is completing coursework for science subjects, this may apply more to him than for John. More than likely, Freddie conducts a designed experiment in completing his BGCSE coursework requirements. In this case, he expects to use strict control over the units (people, objects, or events) in his study. Depending on the nature of his study, he looks at treatment groups and control groups.

Surveys

Surveys are a popular way of obtaining data to satisfy BGCSE coursework requirements. John's research requires the use of a survey. In this case, he samples a group of people, asking questions and recording responses. John's options are mailed surveys, telephone interviews, and personal interviews.

Observation

Alternatively John explores observation. If he chooses this option, he observes the experimental units in their natural setting and records the variable(s) of interest. In the role of observer, John makes no attempt to control any aspects of the experimental units. Examples include job shadowing, mystery shopping, ride-alongs, and call monitoring.

Random Sample

Regardless of the data-collection method used, it is likely that the data will be a sample from some population. If John chooses to apply inferential statistics, he obtains a representative sample. A representative sample exhibits characteristics typical of those possessed by the target population.

The most common way to satisfy the representative sample requirement is to select a random sample. A random sample makes sure that every subset of fixed size in the population has the same chance of being included in the sample.

Let's say John decides to use a survey as a tool to collect data. He thinks about the types of questions to ask. What's his rationale for deciding on particular types of questions? Maybe he bases his decision on

- the number of people to be surveyed;
- how the results will be tabulated; the statistical analysis required;
- the amount of time that respondents have to complete the survey;
- and whether the survey data will be supplemented by other data.

Five question types are commonly used in surveys:

- open-ended
- checklist
- two-way
- ranking
- scaled

John chooses to use any combination of question types in his survey instrument. Generally, it's not advised that he uses more than three different question types in his survey instrument. The last thing he wants to do is to turn the person who is completing the survey off with a confusing survey instrument.

Open Ended

This is a question which may have an unlimited response. For example, "What are the issues that single mothers typically face?"

Checklist

This question type lists a number of items which respondents must select and check off (multiple selections are allowed).

"Which type of neckline do you find more flattering for woman's fashion?"

- round neck
- V-neck turtleneck high neck

Two-Way

This question gives respondents only two choices. For example, "Do you drive a standard shift car?"

- Yes
- No

Ranking

This question type presents a list of items that respondents must rank according to a specified criterion. For example, "Rank the following subjects in order of importance for the job of a human resource manager (write 1 beside the most important and 2 beside the next most important, etc.)."

- math
- English science social studies office procedures

Scaled

This question asks respondents to select numbers or descriptors on a scale to express their opinions. For example, "How many times did you complete your math assignments last month?"

0 1-2 3-4 5-6 6+

Do's of Survey Administration

There are some basic common practices for conducting surveys that John finds useful in following to make sure that he is successful:

- Use a small sample size and try to get all survey sheets returned.
- Leave spaces for people filling in the survey to put in their comments.
- Begin with simple, nonthreatening questions.
- Make sure instructions are clear.
- Conduct the survey in person to a small group if possible and collect all surveys before the people who have completed the survey leave if this is possible.

Explain the following to people filling in the survey before conducting the survey:

- purpose of the survey
- how the information will be used
- how long the survey will take to complete
- how the people filling in the survey will benefit

- deadline for returning survey

Don'ts of Survey Administration

John knows that being aware of the don'ts of conducting a survey helps in preventing him from pitfalls. He makes sure that he does not do any of the following:

- ask too many questions
- use difficult and/or vague language
- use questions that are worded in ways that the people filling in the survey may fear answering correctly
- ask the people filling in the survey to put their name or any information that may be used to identify them on the survey sheet
- make the survey too difficult to complete

Summary as It Relates to Completing Surveys and Your BGCSE Coursework

John familiarizes himself with four different ways of getting the information that he needs for his research. He chooses to use a survey to apply to a random sample that represents the population under investigation for his study. He needs to decide on the question types. He knows about the five different question types to select from. He also knows about what to do—and what not to do—as it relates to survey administration.

Creating the Outline

You must always know what you want.

John's recalls his father's words from years earlier when he saw him last. John now knows what he wants and works toward it every day. He values the outline that Mrs. Davis urged him to create for his coursework project. The outline is the framework for the entire project—what to do, why you do it, and how to do it. John's outline is based on his aim. He will use this outline as his guide. John has broken down his project according to what he needs to do to properly develop his research.

John treasures opening up to Freddie. From there, he meets Freddie's mother and winds up in a strange place called being alive. He's proud of himself. He's learning about some important things.

John thinks about the time he's wasted in the same place, wrangling with the same demons while others move on. He wonders if he should look for his father and rebuild relationships with his mother, brothers, and sister. Until now, he had never wanted to change anything because he didn't know how to deal with change.

For years, he said, "I'm used to the way I am."

Now he understands something new. *I'm forcing myself to look at horizons I've never known. I know how to create an outline for coursework—why can't I create an outline for every aspect of my life and plan my life like a project?*

John's Outline

Step 1
Write the Aim

Workers do their job faster when they use automated records management systems and they like their job. Use internally published data, surveys and interview to support this claim.

How To Do It

- Write a topic sentence
- Write a supporting idea

- Say how and where you will get the accurate and appropriate information that you need to develop your topic sentence and supporting idea

Where To Get The Information

- Review subject-related textbooks, class notes, and knowledge of data collection methods

Step 2
Breakdown aim into topic sentence and supporting idea

Topic sentence: Workers do their job faster
Supporting idea: When they use automated records management systems and they like their job

How To Do It

Breakdown Topic Sentence (Workers do their job faster)

- Find out how much work the average office worker is supposed to do who works in a records management job

Breakdown Supporting Idea (When they use automated records management systems)

- Get as much information about the automated records management system as you can
- Find out about the different types of automated records management systems
- Look at all aspects of automated records management systems
- Describe what automated records management systems are supposed to do

- Explain how automated records management systems help workers to do their job fast

Breakdown Supporting Idea (And they like their job)

- Find out what conditions workers need in place to feel good about their job
- Read up on information on human resources and worker motivation and rewards and recognition to learn why it is important for workers to like their job
- Read up on the relationship between workers attitude toward their job and how fast they do their work

Breakdown Supporting Idea (And they don't like their job)

- Find out what conditions workers usually have in place that contribute to them not liking their job
- Read up on information on human resources and worker motivation and rewards and recognition to learn what usually happens to workers performance and output when they don't like their job
- Read up on information to learn more about the warning signs of worker dissatisfaction
- Read up on the relationship between work place conditions worker attitude and performance

Where To Get The Information

- Review subject-related textbooks, class notes, and knowledge and use of data collection methods

Step 3
Collect data to find out what is supposed to happen and what is really happening

Topic sentence: Workers do their job faster
Supporting idea: When they use automated records management systems and they like their job

How To Do It

Collect Data About Topic Sentence (Workers do their job faster)

- Ask the manager or supervisor to tell you how much work the average office worker is supposed to do who uses an automated records management machine
- Ask the manager or supervisor to tell you how long it should take an office worker to process the information using the system

Collect Data About Supporting Idea (When they use automated records management systems)

- Ask the business to give you information about the automated records management system that they use at their organization
- Ask the business to tell you about the different types of automated records management systems that they use in their organization
- Ask the business to tell you what the automated records management systems are supposed to do at their organization
- Ask the business whether they believe that automated records management systems help workers to do their job faster now as opposed to when they used the manual system

Collect Data About Supporting Idea To Find Out How Workers Feel About Their Job (And they like their job)

- Ask the worker if they know how much work they are supposed to be doing when they use the automated records management system on their job
- Ask the worker if they know how long it should take them to process the information using the system
- Ask the worker to tell you the actual amount of work that they are doing when using the automated records management system on their job
- Ask the worker to tell you how long it is really taking them to process the information using the automated records management system
- Ask the worker if they get recognition from their manager and or supervisor when they receive the desired results on the job
- Ask the worker if they get criticism from their manager and or supervisor when they do not achieve the desired results on the job
- Ask the worker if they have the tools, equipment and resources to achieve the desired results on the job
- Ask the worker what obstacles stop them from performing on their job in they way that they should (i.e. technology, training, skills, more staff etc.)

Where To Get The Information

- Obtain this information from the business along with knowledge and use of data collection methods

Step 4
Identify the difference between what the worker is supposed to do and what they are doing

How To Do It

- Look at the data from your survey or interview and see if there is a difference between what should be happening and what is actually happening when it comes to workers who use automated systems

Where To Get The Information

- Survey, Interview, Internet etc.

Step 5
Find the root cause behind what is happening and what is supposed to be happening

How To Do It

- Look at the responses to the questions in your survey questionnaire where you asked the worker for information about the conditions on their job
- Look at the responses to the questions where you asked the worker about how they feel about their job
- Look at the responses to the questions where you asked the worker about the output that they produce on the job while using the automated records management system
- Evaluate by making a judgment based on the information that you pull from the survey to see what is causing the difference between what is happening and what is supposed to be happening

in terms of the amount of work that the worker is producing on the job as it relates to the worker's attitude
- Support your judgment and opinion with reason and evidence

Where To Get The Information

- Review subject-related textbooks, class notes, and knowledge and use of data collection methods

Step 6
Make a decision

How To Do It

- Make a decision based on the information that you put together so far
- Make sure that your decision is in line with your argument and aim

Where To Get The Information

- Review subject-related textbooks, class notes, and knowledge and use of data collection methods

Step 7
Present your draft outline

How To Do It

- Put your outline together for presentation according to the format presented in the Guide to Coursework Contents
- Pay attention to the layout
- Include explanation of any diagrams and choice of methods for presenting your data

Where To Get The Information

- Survey, Interview, Internet etc.

Estimating How Long it Will Take to Complete Each Task in the Outline

Mrs. Davis is nearing the wrap-up of a weekly tutoring session with Freddie and John. She says

"When you estimate the amount of time that it will take to complete each task in the outline, you are looking at the number of hours or days. Make sure and include all the time that will pass from the beginning of the task until the work is completed."

"How am I supposed to know all the time that will pass from the beginning of the task until the work is completed?"

"For this information, John, rely on people who are most knowledgeable about the tasks you are trying to estimate. They will help with this process. Take a few moments to put the times for completing the tasks next to the tasks in your outline."

Step 1
Write the aim—5 days

Step 2
Breakdown aim into topic sentence and supporting idea—10 days

Step 3
Collect data to find out what is supposed to happen and what is really happening—10 days

Step 4
Identify the difference between what the worker is supposed to do and what they are doing—10 days

Step 5
Find the root cause behind what is happening and what is supposed to be happening—10 days

Step 6
Make a decision—10 days

Step 7
Present your draft outline—10 days

Creating a Schedule

"John, I'm very proud of you. Now that you have put the times beside the tasks that you must complete in your outline, you have your schedule. I was hoping you would catch on fast based on how I've seen you develop—and you are certainly living up to my expectations. I'm rushing off to my next meeting and only have five minutes to get there. Freddie will review quality with you, and I will be back shortly to answer any questions you may have. See you again soon."

When Mrs. Davis leaves, Freddie takes the lead.

Focusing on Quality

"John, imagine that you're involved in a situation. You expect a certain outcome. Your mind is geared up—and your excitement and anticipation levels are at an all-time high—when the moment of truth arrives, what you expect to get is so far removed from what you actually get that you can't believe your eyes."

"Freddie, it's coincidental that you use that example. I'm still dealing with a situation like what you describe. I still can't get over my report card last semester."

"There's no such thing as coincidence, John. Events are always linked—whether you realize it or not. You relate to this experience—and you fundamentally understand the importance of quality."

Freddie defines quality as meeting the Ministry of Education's expectations for coursework.

"There are three costs associated with quality," Freddie says. "Prevention costs, appraisal costs, and failure costs. Prevention costs are the costs that come with satisfying customer requirements by producing a document without errors. These costs come early in the process and include training and internal review."

"How are training and internal review considered costs?" John asks.

"Well, someone has to spend money for you to learn how to do something correctly. My mummy pays for extra classes for me to learn for me to produce quality work at the end of the day. This is prevention cost. She doesn't leave everything up to the tutor though; she reviews my work and assignments. She is accountable—and I am responsible.

"Appraisal costs are the costs that you pay to examine the document, making certain that requirements are met. In the working world, appraisal costs might include costs that come with inspections or testing. You have to pay for inspectors, you know."

"I didn't know you had to pay for inspectors. That's news to me."

"Failure costs are what it costs when things don't go according to plan. Failure costs are also known as the cost of poor quality. Internal failure costs result when requirements are not met while your coursework is still in your control. Internal failure costs may include corrective action, rework and scrapping. External failure costs occur when your coursework has reached the reviewer—who determines that the requirements are not met. Costs associated with external failure costs might include a failing grade."

"I must be experiencing failure costs."

"Why do you say that, John?"

"I'm repeating, you know."

"I know." Freddie looks John directly in the eyes. "No matter how many detours and adjustments you make, you keep moving toward your goals. Overcome the obstacles and move on."

Communicating Effectively

Weeks pass. John rekindles his relationship with his father. On the long summer nights when the heat is unbearable in the house, they sit outside under the tree. John updates his dad on his life.

During one of the conversations, John's father says, "I had a really good job in one of the leading banks downtown; it was a high-paying job. I was a manager. That was a big-time position—it still is, as a matter of fact. I made sure that you and your brothers and your sister had really nice things. Your mother had lots of jewelry. I used to like to see her looking pretty.

"One day, my whole life fell apart—right in front of my face. I took sick. I almost died. I lost my job. I lost it all. Everything was destroyed. I never liked to talk to people. I don't like people to be all up in my business. You know what I mean?"

John nods, and his eyes fill with water.

"I find other ways to earn a living now. I do odd jobs. I don't feel like I could do much of anything anymore. I'm afraid to go back into the mainstream out of fear of losing everything again."

"Why don't you talk to someone, Daddy? I know there are plenty people around who can—and will—help you."

The two are silent. John senses fear in the air—even though no one says anything.

"Once you get to the point where I am, son, there's no turning back."

"Why not think about moving forward?" John asks. "You can turn yourself around. I'm studying about communication and how importance it is to talk to people who have an interest in you and what you are working on—who could help you to make or break it—find out what they need from you so you can understand how to meet their needs. We all need each other. We need to know what we need, who we need it from, when we need it, and where to go to get it."

"You should take a break from studying those books and pay more attention to life, son."

"And you should read more books. Like I said, I'm learning that in project management communication is the key. You have to know about the types of information that the people need who will help you, the way that they want you to communicate the information to them, and how often the information should be given out.

"You have to make sure that your communication is efficient and effective. Effective communication means that information is provided in the right way, at the right time, and with the right impact. Efficient communication means that you only give out the information that is needed."

"That sounds important, but I'm still not sure why you're telling me this, boy. I'm telling you about how my life is a complete failure— and you're telling me about a communication plan that you read about in some book. Are you trying to tell me that I need to create a communication plan for my life?"

"Boy, are you testing me?"

"I don't mean to be persistent, Daddy. I apologize. I'm now willing to study things deeply to achieve the vision I have for my life. I understand that I can manage my life like a project—and that I have to build stronger relationships with others, communicate effectively, and focus more on the needs of others and not just my needs."

His father does not respond.

"My best friend Freddie tells me that there is no such thing as coincidence. I believe that. As you told me your story, I read the codes and saw my life. I don't have to live your experience anymore; you've already lived it."

John's father nods, hanging his head.

"I'd like it if you would share more of your experiences with me so I can learn through you. You seem old and wise," John says.

"And maybe I need to read your books."

The two embrace.

Reducing the Risk

Mrs. Davis is busy, but she assigns John some reading from one of her project management magazines.

Flipping through the pages, John comes across an article about risk that gets his attention. The article explains that risks are always present in our lives—and a project is no exception.

The article describes risk as an uncertain event or condition that, if it occurs, may seriously affect the project outcome. A risk event may have one or more causes; if it occurs, it may have one or more impacts. A cause may be a requirement, an assumption, a constraint, or a condition that creates the possibility of a positive or negative outcome.

John learns that risk management addresses uncertainty in project estimates and assumptions. He realizes that the more he knows about risks and their impacts beforehand, the better equipped he would be to handle a risk when it occurs.

Not all risks are bad. That's news to his ears. Risks may present future opportunities as well as future threats. Known risks are the ones that he identifies and analyzes, making it possible to respond promptly to those risks. Unknown risks, on the other hand, cannot be managed beforehand, which suggests that he should create a backup plan. When a risk event occurs, it ceases to become uncertain; it is now an issue.

John's goal is to manage risk. The thing is, risks cannot be managed unless they are first identified. John's objective is to identify risks to the maximum extent that it is possible. He already wrote some risks down when he was completing his start up checklist. At the time he identifies the risk, he also identifies potential responses. As he records the possible responses he determines the instances where immediate action is appropriate.

Managing The List of People to Talk to

As John moves through project planning, he feels the need to always create effective ways of keeping the people on the list to talk to engaged in his project, managing the expectations he has for them and their expectations for him. John's ultimate goal is to achieve the coursework objectives and he cannot do it alone.

With his project management planning processes complete, John feels accomplished. There's still much work to do. With the deadlines fast approaching, John moves to make it happen.

Key Points to Remember

- An outline is the framework for the entire coursework.
- Information from the start up checklist is used when creating an outline.
- Base your choice of topic on your BGCSE coursework requirement.
- Your topic should include material that you have already covered as a part of your BGCSE coursework syllabus.
- Identifying your aim provides structure for your research upfront.
- Without an aim, you will not know where your research is headed—or when you have arrived at your desired outcome.
- Objectives are tactics that you use to achieve your aim.
- Statistics deal with collecting, classifying, summarizing, organizing, analyzing, and interpreting numerical data.
- The BGCSE coursework requires students to know how to properly present and describe information, draw conclusions about large populations based only on information obtained through samples, improve processes, and obtain reliable forecasts.
- Sampling is the process of selecting data from a larger set of data whose characteristics we wish to estimate as a part of our BGCSE coursework requirements.

- The two broad areas of statistics are classified as descriptive and inferential.
- Descriptive statistics uses numerical and graphical methods to look for patterns in a data set, to summarize the information revealed in a data set, and to present that information in a convenient form.
- Inferential statistics use sample data to make estimates, decisions, predictions, or other generalizations about a larger set of data.
- A population is a set of units (usually people, objects, transactions, or events) that we are interested in studying.
- When we study a population, we focus on one or more characteristics or properties of the units in the population. We call these characteristics variables.
- Measurement is the process that we use to assign numbers to variables of individual population units.
- Studying a subset or portion of the population is called sampling.
- Reliability is a measure of how good the inference is.
- A statement about the degree of uncertainty associated with the statistical inference should be used as a measure of reliability.
- Quantitative data is data measured on a naturally occurring numerical scale.
- Qualitative data cannot be measured on a natural numerical scale.
- Generally you may obtain data in four different ways (published source, a designed experiment, a survey, or observation).
- Published data is collected and presented in a published source.
- If you use a designed experiment, you will be expected to use strict control over the units (people, objects, or events) in your study.
- A survey is a popular way of obtaining data to satisfy your BGCSE coursework requirement.
- Observation requires that you observe the experimental units in their natural settings and record the variable(s) of interest.
- A representative sample exhibits characteristics typical of those that the target population has.

- The most common way to satisfy the representative sample is to select a random sample.
- A random sample makes sure that every subset of fixed size in the population has the same chance of being included in the sample.
- The five types of questions that are commonly used in surveys are open-ended, checklist, two-way, ranking, and scaled questions.
- You should begin your survey with simple, nonthreatening questions.
- You should not use difficult or vague language in a survey.
- The description of each task to complete the outline should begin with a verb.
- Activity duration estimates are presented as the number of work periods needed to complete a task.
- Work periods may be expressed in hours, days, or months.
- When planning quality, identify quality requirements or standards for the project and product.
- Consider the trade-off of the cost of quality. It is cheaper and more efficient to prevent defects in the first place than to spend time and money fixing them later.
- Three costs associated with the cost of quality are prevention costs, appraisal costs, and failure costs.
- Appraisal costs are the costs you have to pay to examine the product or process.
- Failure costs are what it costs when things do not go according to plan.
- Internal failure costs result when the Ministry of Education's requirements are not satisfied while the coursework is still in your control.
- External failure costs occur when the coursework has reached Ministry of Education, and they determine that the requirements are not met.
- Your communication plan should document the approach you will take to make sure you have efficient and effective communication with the people on your list to talk to.

- Effective communication means that information is provided in the right format at the right time and with the right impact.
- Efficient communication means that you provide only the necessary information.
- A risk is an uncertain event or condition that, if it occurs, has an effect on at least one aspect of the coursework project.
- A risk event may have one or more causes, and if it occurs, it may have one or more impacts.
- Not all risks are bad.
- Risks may present future opportunities as well as future threats to the project.
- When a risk event occurs, it ceases to become uncertain.
- A risk cannot be managed unless it is first identified.
- Identifying risks is an ongoing process.
- Brainstorming and interviewing subject matter experts, and people with previous experience writing BGCSE coursework are great ways to collect high-quality information about risks.
- One of your goals for identifying risks is to come away with enough information to build a list of the risks that you identified, where the risks are described in as much detail as is reasonable.

Applying to the Next Project

Discussion Questions

1. What rationale should you use for choosing your BGCSE coursework topic?
2. What are some things that you should consider when choosing an organization to investigate as a part of your BGCSE coursework requirements?
3. What is the purpose of the aim?
4. What should be included as a part of the aim?
5. What are some components that make up a strong aim?

6. Why would you need data collection instruments when completing your BGCSE coursework?

7. What are some examples of action verbs that may be included in an objective statement?

8. What is the definition of statistics?

9. Why is it important to gather statistical data?

10. Why are knowledge and skill in statistical concepts necessary for BGCSE coursework completion?

11. What is the difference between descriptive and inferential statistics?

12. What are the four elements of descriptive statistical problems?

13. What is meant by sampling?

14. What are five elements of inferential statistical problems?

15. What is the definition of a population?

16. Why do we focus on variables when we study a population?

17. Why is measurement important?

18. How do we define reliability?

19. What are the different types of data?

20. What are the four methods for obtaining data?

21. What is the definition of published data?

22. How do you conduct a designed experiment?

23. What are some methods for collecting data with a survey?

24. What must you not do when collecting data using the observation method?

25. What is the best way to obtain a representative sample?

26. What are five different question types?

27. What are four do's of survey administration?

28. What are four don'ts of survey administration?

29. What are the steps in breaking down the aim?

30. What would be the benefit of breaking down the aim?

31. What is meant by activities?

32. Why is it important to complete all activities in support of your aim?

33. How do you determine what resources you may need to complete each activity?

34. How do you determine how long it will take to complete each activity?
35. What is meant by quality?
36. What does the process of ensuring quality entail?
37. How can you follow the steps for ensuring quality?
38. How do you determine what quality requirements are necessary to complete each activity?
39. What may happen to your coursework in the absence of effective communication?
40. What is meant by project risk?
41. What impact may risk have on your coursework?
42. Why is it important to properly identify risks that may impact your coursework?
43. What can happen if you fail to properly identify risks that may impact your coursework?
44. What are some ways to identify risks that may impact your coursework?

Debrief Questions

1. What are the key learning points?
2. What information was new to you?
3. What concepts will you apply in the future? When?
4. What challenges do you anticipate may limit your ability to apply the concepts?
5. What needs to be in place to overcome these challenges?
6. Who would you recommend these concepts to and why?

Activity

The following activity may be completed individually or in a small group to assess your comprehension.

1. Answer the discussion questions.

2. Answer the debrief questions.
3. Create a survey instrument (for mail, telephone interviews, or in-person interviews).
4. Test the tool by giving it to a small representative sample (maybe five people).
5. Review.
6. Give your survey tool to the sample population under investigation.
7. Analyze the data.
8. Compile the data in an appropriate format to support analysis (chart, graph, table, or written categorized summary).
9. Use the data to support a decision in line with argument and aim.

CHAPTER 3

MAKING IT HAPPEN

After studying this chapter, you should be able to

Gathering Data

- state the four categories that information about an organization may come from;
- explain the kind of information that may be included in the general information category;
- describe the kind of information that may be included in the category that describes factors external to the organization;
- highlight the information that is included in the category that describes factors related to the internal operations of the organization;
- explain the kind of information that may be included in the category that describes factors related to human performance category;
- state five examples of questions that may be asked in each of the four respective categories that information about an organization may come from;
- identify five things that you should familiarize yourself with before going on your appointment;
- state the benefits of categorizing questions;
- list and describe some preparation steps for successful meetings;
- cite the ways that information may be presented to stakeholders on a project;

Updating the People on Your List to Talk to

- explain the importance of updating the people on your list of people to talk to;

Managing Expectations

- describe what is meant by managing expectations;

Monitoring and Controlling Schedule

- explain the importance of monitoring and controlling the project;
- list and describe some activities that may be included as a part of monitoring and controlling the project;

Reporting Performance

- explain the importance of reporting performance;

Controlling Risks

- state the importance of monitoring and controlling risks; and
- explain how risks are monitored and controlled in a project.

Gathering Data

John finishes the project planning processes and begins executing them. He thinks about gathering data and reflects on suspense thriller movies where there's a "person of interest" under investigation. The detective conducts background checks. Depending on the circumstances, these background checks may be quite extensive, and they may include getting information about an individual's primary, secondary, and high school performance—and their lives and people they hung out with.

John applies the same principles of investigation to getting information about the organization of interest for his BGCSE coursework. He looks at the organization using a big picture approach. This includes getting general information about the business, looking at factors outside of the business, factors relating to internal operations, and factors relating to human performance. He knows that general information about the business includes

- business name;
- address;
- contact information (phone, cell, e-mail, post office box, etc.);
- business owner;
- years in business; and
- locations.

Businesses often have websites or published data; he gets general information about the business with little effort. He considers confirming the accuracy of the general information—and getting a little more information or insight into the business by asking relevant questions in the form of surveys or interviews. John's goal is to get a good understanding of the business's present state. This starts with getting general information.

Businesses do not operate in vacuums. External environmental factors strongly influence a business's internal state of affairs. In researching the business under investigation, John also needs to get information about the following as it relates to the environment that the business operates in:

- economic conditions
- competition
- government regulations
- demographics
- changing customer expectations

- legislation

Just as with any other living, breathing thing, what goes on outside impacts what happens inside within businesses. John knows that thoroughly investigating businesses often includes looking at information such as operational and/or strategic goals for units or departments. Reports normally capture information presented below:

- growth in market share
- reduction in waste
- increase in sales
- customer service metrics

Then, of course, there's the human element. John knows that people are at the heart of any business. Looking at what's happening outside of the business and what's happening inside of the business includes investigating what's happening with the people working in the business. Investigating human components requires that he investigates the on-the-job behavioral requirements and practices of people who are performing specific jobs. In this instance, he needs to get the kind of information that describes what people produce through their day-to-day performance if the needs of the business are to be met. He also needs to get information that describes the best practices by which these results are produced. He outlines some sample questions that he considers asking to collect general information as well as information from the external environment, internal environment, and human performance.

Sample Questions for Data Gathering—General Information

The following are some sample questions that John may ask to obtain general information about the business:

- What is the name of your business?

- What is your address?
- How can I contact your business (phone, cell, e-mail, post office box)?
- What is the name of the business owner?
- How many years has the business been in operation?
- How many locations are there—and where are they?

Sample Questions for Data Gathering—External Environment

The following are some sample questions that John may ask to obtain information about the external environment within the business:

- What industry is your business classified under?
- Where do businesses within this industry get their products or services?
- Who are the suppliers?
- Are suppliers local, regional, or international?
- What is the availability of suppliers?
- What is the life stage of the industry that your business operates in (emergent, mature, or declining)?
- Are there substitute products?
- How many primary products are there?
- Are these products difficult to make—and if so, why?
- Would it be difficult to invent or produce a substitute—and if so, why?
- How would you describe the dependence on other industries (supply dependencies, sales dependence)?
- Is this industry seasonal—and if so, during which period?
- How does this industry move with economic changes (in tandem, counter, or no change)?
- What are the expectations of change in local, regional, or national regulations that might affect this industry?

Sample Questions for Data Gathering—Internal Environment

The following are some sample questions that John may ask to obtain information about the internal environment within the business:

- What is currently going on in your business?
- What are your major business objectives for the next twelve months?
- Why are these objectives important to focus on at this time?
- What are the driving forces behind these objectives?
- What indicators or metrics are you using to measure success (both desired and current results)?
- What strategies are in place to achieve these results?
- What factors outside of the organization will challenge the achievement of this goal?
- What factors outside of the organization will encourage success?
- What should your production output be?
- What is your production output?
- What are your sales goals for the year?
- What are your actual sales results for this year?
- What are the primary reasons why current output is below goal/target?
- What is the standard rate for acceptable wastage?
- What is the current wastage rate?
- Why is the wastage rate increasing or decreasing?
- What would you expect for levels of inventory, receivables, and payables?
- What is your present strategy for sales and marketing?
- How do you measure the impact of your present sales and marketing strategy?
- What is the business source of suppliers (local, regional, or international)?
- What is the availability of suppliers for your business?
- Do you plan to add or change locations in the future? Why or why not?

- Do you plan to purchase new premises?
- Do you plan to add or decrease staff?
- What kind of a year are you having financially?
- How does that compare with previous years?
- What are your records management needs?
- How would you describe your file classification system?
- What should staff do when responding to customer complaints?
- How does staff manage customer complaints now?
- How does your exemplary salesperson close a sale?
- What does the typical salesperson do when closing a sale?

Sample Questions for Data Gathering—Human Performance

The following are some sample questions that John may ask to obtain information about the factors that relate to human performance within the business:

- What is the reason for the gap between what the staff should be doing and what the staff is actually doing?
- Why are the sales officers not closing sales at the desired percentage rate?
- What conditions could prevent employees from achieving required targets?

John consults his tip sheet on ways to improve response rates from questionnaires and surveys. This is a treasure from Mrs. Davis.

Improving the Response Rate for Questionnaires and Surveys

Provide Advance Communication

If appropriate and feasible, respondents should receive advance communication about the requirement to complete a questionnaire. This minimizes resistance to the process, provides an opportunity to explain the circumstances surrounding the evaluation in more detail, and positions the follow-up evaluation as an important part of the process—and not just an add-on activity.

Communicate the Purpose

Respondents should understand the reason for the questionnaire. Respondents should know if the evaluation is included as a part of an ongoing process or as a special request.

Explain Who Will See the Data

It is important for respondents to know who will see the data and the results of the questionnaire. If the questionnaire is anonymous, the steps that will be taken to ensure anonymity should be clearly communicated to the respondents. Respondents should know if senior executives will see the combined results of the study.

Describe the Data-Integration Process

Respondents should understand how the questionnaire results will be combined with other data, if applicable. The questionnaire may only be one of the data-collection methods used. Respondents should know how the data is weighted and included into the final report.

Keep the Questionnaire as Simple as Possible

A simplified approach should always be the goal when creating questionnaires. When questions are developed and finalized, every effort should be made to keep the questionnaire as simple and brief as possible.

Simplify the Response Process

It should be easy to respond to the questionnaire. If it is easier, an e-mail system may be used for response. In other instances, questionnaires may be collected by a responsible party.

Use Management Support

Management involvement is critical to response rate success. Managers may distribute the questionnaires, refer to the questionnaires in the staff meetings, follow-up to see if the questionnaires are completed, and generally show support for completing the questionnaires. When management demonstrates this level of engagement, some respondents may provide usable data.

Let Respondents Know They Are Part of a Sample

If appropriate, respondents should know that they are part of a carefully selected sample and that their input will be used to make decisions regarding a much larger target audience. This action often appeals to a sense of responsibility for respondents to provide usable, accurate data for the questionnaire.

Use Follow-Up Reminders

A follow-up reminder should be sent one week after the questionnaire is received—and another sent two weeks after it is received. Depending on the questionnaire and the situation, these times may be adjusted. Send reminders to the identified point person in the business who has assumed the role of supporting questionnaire completion.

Consider Keeping Input Anonymous

Anonymous data is often more objective. If respondents believe their input is anonymous, they may be more inclined to be constructive and more honest in their feedback—and response rates will generally be higher.

Treat Data with Confidence

Confidentiality is an important part of the process. A confidentiality statement may be included, indicating that respondent names and identities will not be revealed to anyone other than the data collectors and those involved in analyzing the data. In some instances, it may be appropriate to indicate who will actually see the raw data. Include specific steps taken to ensure data confidentiality.

Explain How Long the Questionnaire Takes to Complete

Respondents often appreciate having a realistic understanding of how long it may take them to provide the data. It may be frustrating to the respondent if the time presented for completing the questionnaire is grossly underestimated.

Remember

Always be governed by the requirements of the respective subject area that your coursework is associated with. If your BGCSE subject area does not require that you investigate an organization as a part of your coursework requirements, these sections that relate to such investigation will be irrelevant to you at this time.

Conducting Meetings

John is nervous. Going into new territories or new environments makes him uneasy. He realizes that he doesn't know what's happening, where to go for what, and who to speak to for the information and resources he needs. He's been talking to his father a lot recently and has gotten good tips and protocol for acceptable behavior in formal office settings.

John's father says, "Conducting a paper-based, telephone, or in-person survey can be an unsettling experience. For you, it is most likely new territory that puts you in a new environment. Minimize the scary emotions that come with experiencing new environments by familiarizing yourself with some key things before your appointment."

John's father prepares with him, ensuring that John is familiar with the subject and/or topic under investigating. "This increases your level of confidence and gives you a good background for asking spin-off questions from the ones that you have prepared in advance. Demonstrating confidence leaves the respondent with a good impression of you—and the school you represent."

John captures a list of things that his father advises him to become familiar with when investigating businesses.

- a business model for the organization
- how revenues and profits are generated
- how the organization provides value to its customers
- operational metrics used to measure the health of the organization including goals and actual results

- the balance sheet for the organization, indicating assets, liabilities, and equity the strategic plan and initiatives implemented to support the organization's goals and requirements
- core processes used to fulfill the business's mission and achieve results (order fulfillment process, sales and marketing process, and records management)
- values and cultural norms
- customer profiles for the business's products and services level of maturity of the business and its products and services
- primary competitors and competitive pressures that the organization is facing
- marketplace where the organization competes
- businesses that are key players in the market
- differentiators of the business under investigation from others in the same industry forces and factors that affect the marketplace (outside the control of the business but may challenge its success)
- governmental regulatory requirements
- primary market segments that are sources for current and future customers for the industry and business under investigation
- global factors that impact the industry
- financial and nonfinancial benchmarks for businesses in the industry that are—or can be—used for comparison

John recalls his subject teacher telling the class that regardless of the subject area, as a general rule, categorizing questions is of benefit whether conducting a written or an oral survey. Obvious benefits of categorizing questions are strong organization, structure, and flow to the interview or questionnaire. Categorizing questions allows John to identify opportunities to ask spin-off questions.

He sees other advantages to categorizing questions as support in helping him gather comprehensive demographic information. It helps him obtain information efficiently, which he uses to show up gaps between what is, versus what should be as it relates to his topic under investigation.

Finally, categorizing questions helps John organize the data he gets from the survey. The data reveals the kind of information that makes it possible to chart and/or graph responses. Additionally, the data provides him with the necessary support to make a decision in line with his aim.

John's father still travels, but he hangs around the house more often. John enjoys having him around and finds that he spends less time with Freddie and his mother and more time learning from his father. Freddie was right when he pointed out that there's no such thing as coincidence.

I've learned from Mrs. Davis, I've learned from Freddie, and I've learned from my teachers. I'm learning some things from my father now.

John's father says, "Son, going into this business to carry out this research will test your every step. If it's in time, you'll make it through. You're familiar with the business and its territory. We've gone through that repeatedly. You know your aim, topic sentence and supporting idea—and you've categorized your questions. You're almost ready to conduct your survey."

- Create the objective of the meeting and the opening remarks.
- Practice the opening statement you will use with the person you are interviewing.
- State the purpose for the meeting (state the information that you want to get).
- Ask the person who you are interviewing to tell you what they want to get out of the interview.
- Agree on the purpose (s) and time frame for the interview.
- Explain the format of the interview and confirm agreement.
- State what actions will be taken after the interview.
- Begin the conversation by sharing what you know about the business and get them to confirm whether your information is accurate or not.
- Summarize what you know about the business or topic, based on your research, or begin by asking general questions.
- Don't come to a decision in the interview. Focus on what is happening at the time.
- Respect the business person's time and confidential information.
- Conclude the meeting graciously.

- Ask the business person who you are interviewing if you can get in contact with them in the future if you need to clarify any additional information.

Updating The List of People to Talk to

"I need help," John says with bloodshot eyes and dark circles under them.

John's father looks at his son. The boy looks as tired as he does. "Son, sit down. I want to talk to you this morning because I've been in and out—and I haven't been able to catch up with you for days. Update me on your teacher's reaction to the information you updated her on last week." He rubs his hands wearily over his eyes.

"Actually, I'm ashamed to admit it, but I forgot to update my teacher on my progress last week. I know I should have told you sooner, but I just could not build up the courage to bring it to your attention—and besides, you've been in and out."

"Boy, don't run me hot!" John's heart sinks. "I don't like this feeling that I am experiencing right now. This is not a good feeling, especially if this is a situation where we may have prevented an outcome or reduced the consequences of some actions if I had known about this important information in advance. You do realize that failing to make sure that the right information is distributed to the people on the project can bring the project to a screeching halt and jeopardize everything that we've been working toward for months. What do I need to know?" He begins writing on a blank page in his notebook.

John weighs the pros and cons of telling the truth and lying and decides to give his father the benefit of the truth.

His father smiles; it's not a pretty expression . . . more dreary than joyful. "We're in big trouble. These are the kinds of things that got me in trouble on my job. I can't believe that you're falling into the same trap as me, John. Giving out information and updating people on the list of people you need to talk to according to the agreements that you made is living up to your word."

"What stopped you from updating your teacher?"

"I didn't know what to do," John says.

John's father adds a whole lot of sugar to his coffee. "I'll explain a bit about communication skills to help educate you about giving out project information." He covers his mouth and coughs repeatedly. Once his hacking fit is under control, he continues, "Communication skills have to be some of the most important skills you can have—even more important than technical skills. Good communication skills encourage an open, trusting environment—and are an asset."

"This is all new for me."

"Didn't they teach you this in school last year?"

"Last year? I hardly went to school last year. I am repeating last year this year—and they still didn't teach me any of this. I'm learning firsthand from you right here and now."

John's father chuckles. There's no such thing as coincidence. This story sounds dangerously close to the ones he told when he was his son's age. He's too tired to take his son on and doesn't want to be derailed. He raises his chin and says, "You need to start doing what you are supposed to do and do it right now."

John sighs. "I was thinking I could start working on the update for my teacher after I come home from work."

"From work? You planning on putting selling phone cards in front of your schoolwork? Boy, you must be crazy. Sell me one five-dollar card so you can ease your tension and feel like you made a sale today—and then get in that room and do your schoolwork before I roll up on you."

"I didn't have anything else to do today . . . like relax, play games, listen to music, or anything boring like that. I was always planning on doing schoolwork all day on Saturday. Okay, then. I'm right on it, sir."

His father turns away, ignoring him.

Managing Expectations

The hostess whispers, "We can squeeze a seat for you over here in the holding room. You know its standing room only, but we're trying to fit everyone in."

The no-frills, cubicle-sized enclosure referred to as the holding room is designed to give invited guests a claustrophobic feeling. And it's most effective. With nothing to look at but the beige paint on the walls, nothing to sit on but the white aluminum folding chairs, and the temperature raised at least thirty degrees above normal, the occupants have the snug, cozy feeling usually associated with an overcrowded elevator.

"Raise your spirits, family," an unfamiliar voice says. "Just concentrate on the keynote speaker—and you'll get out of here soon."

He turns toward the voice and says, "Thanks. I know there's some reason why I paid five dollars for this field trip that the guidance counselor requires for all BGCSE coursework students. I just don't know what the reason is yet."

"Quiet!" an irritated voice exclaims.

John turns and becomes serious about taking in the information on managing stakeholder expectations.

He learns that managing expectations is the process of communicating and working with the people who you need to help you to succeed. You must always remember to meet their needs and address issues as they occur. Managing expectations involves communication activities directed toward the people on the list of people to talk to. You need to influence their expectations, address concerns, and resolve issues. This may include

- actively managing expectations to increase the likelihood that your coursework will be accepted;
- addressing concerns that have not become issues yet, usually related to the anticipation of future problems;
- uncovering and discussing concerns and assessing risks; and
- clarifying and resolving identified issues.

Actively managing expectations decreases the risk that the coursework project will fail to meet its goals and objectives due to unresolved issues. It also limits disruptions during the project.

Monitoring and Controlling Schedule

John is familiar with the saying that when the cat's away, the entire operation breaks down. Well, that's a modified version of the saying, but I'm sure you get the point. When something—or someone, for that matter—is left unattended for too long, things tend to get out and bad.

John learns that monitoring and controlling the project work is the process of tracking, reviewing, and regulating the progress while meeting the performance objectives defined in your outline. This includes measuring project performance, figuring out what is not going according to the outline, and getting your project back on track if things get out of hand. This makes sense to John.

Monitoring includes collecting, measuring, and distributing project information and assessing measurements and trends that affect project improvement. He understands that continuous monitoring gives insight into the health of the project and identifies any areas that require special attention.

Control includes determining corrective or preventive actions or re-planning and following up on action plans that determine if the actions taken resolve the issue. He learns that monitoring and controlling project work is concerned with

- comparing actual project performance with the outline;
- assessing performance to determine whether any corrective or preventive actions are necessary—and recommending those actions as necessary; and
- identifying new risks and analyzing, tracking, and monitoring existing project risks to make sure the risks are identified, their status is reported, and appropriate risk response plans are being executed.

Reporting Performance

John is sweating bullets as he approaches his father to discuss his performance; he is aware of his neglect in updating his teacher on his coursework project.

John wants to manage his BGCSE coursework project well and avoid the need for more bullet sweating. To ensure this, he needs to report on the project's performance. In the workplace—as well as in school—performance compares to the standard. The same holds true for projects. Performance reporting involves collecting information about coursework project progress and project accomplishments and reporting them to the people on the list of people you need to talk to. This is what John was asked to do. His failure to report to his father tipped him off that the task remained outstanding.

Controlling Risks

Monitoring and controlling risks involves implementing response plans, tracking and monitoring identified risks, and identifying and responding to new risks as they occur during the project.

John reads about risks in a popular project management journal and learns that he should continuously monitor the project work for new, changing, and outdated risks. Monitoring and controlling risks requires the use of performance information generated during project execution.

Some of the other purposes that John has for monitoring and controlling risk is to determine whether his earlier assumptions are still valid or if the analysis showing an assessed risks has changed or can be retired. Monitoring and controlling risk involves choosing alternative strategies, executing a fallback plan, taking corrective action, and modifying the outline.

Once the processes required to start, plan, execute, and monitor and control John's BGCSE coursework project are complete, all that's left is to officially close the project.

Key Points to Remember

- Take a big picture approach when looking at the business that you will investigate as a part of your BGCSE coursework requirement.
- Looking at the business in an overall way includes getting general information about the business—and looking at factors external to the organization, factors related to internal operations of the organization, and factors related to human performance.
- General information about the business includes the business name, address, owner, and years in business.
- Often if the company has a website or publishes data, general information about the business may be obtained easily.
- Your purpose for investigating this business is to support a stated aim that you wrote based on the BGCSE coursework subject requirements.
- Your goal is to get a good understanding of the present state of the business, and it begins with getting general information.
- The internal state of affairs within a business is strongly influenced by what goes on outside of the business.
- A thorough investigation of the business may include the need to look at information such as operational and/or strategic goals for a unit or department.
- Information that relates to the operational and/or strategic goals for a unit or department within a business may also include growth in market share, reduction in waste, increase in sales, and customer service metrics.
- What is happening outside of the business and what is happening inside of the business cannot be looked at independently of investigating what is happening with people who work in the business.
- Investigating the human component in the business requires investigating on-the-job behavioral requirements and practices of people who are performing specific jobs.

- Conducting a paper-based, telephone, or in-person survey can be an unsettling experience because the new territory puts you in a new environment.
- Minimize the scary emotions that come with experiencing new environments by familiarizing yourself with some key things before your appointment.
- Familiarizing yourself with the business under investigation increases your level of confidence and gives you a good background for asking spin-off questions.
- You may wish to become familiar with cultural norms and values as they relate to the business under investigation.
- One obvious benefit of categorizing questions when conducting a survey is that it promotes strong organization, structure, and flow of the interview or questionnaire.
- Categorizing questions also helps when organizing the data that you obtain through the survey instrument.
- The data should reveal information that makes it possible to chart and/or graph responses.
- Additionally, the data should provide you with the necessary support to your aim.
- Be sure to properly prepare for your meeting.
- Distributing information is the process of making relevant information available to the people on your list of people to talk to as planned.
- Communication skills are one of the most important skills a project manager can have.
- Managing expectations is the process of communicating and working with the people on the list of people to talk to, to meet their needs, addressing issues as they occur.
- Monitoring and controlling the project focuses on measuring project performance to identify differences from the outline and get the project back on track.
- Monitoring the project includes collecting, measuring, and distributing project information and assessing measurements and trends that affect the project.

- Control includes determining corrective or preventive actions or re-planning and following up on action plans to determine if the actions taken resolved the performance issue.
- Always remember to update the people on the list of people to talk to about the changes that are being made and their potential results.
- Monitoring and controlling risks requires putting in place response plans, tracking and monitoring identified risks, and identifying and responding to new risks as they occur.
- Continually monitor project work for new, changing, and outdated risks.
- Monitoring and controlling risks may involve choosing alternative strategies, executing a fallback plan, taking corrective action, and modifying the outline.

Applying to the Next Project

Discussion Questions

1. What are the four categories that information about a business may come from?
2. What kind of information may be included in the general information category?
3. What kind of information may be included in the category that describes factors outside of the business?
4. What kind of information may be included in the category that describes factors related to the internal operations of the business?
5. What kind of information may be included in the category that describes factors related to the human performance category?
6. What are five questions that may be asked in the four categories that information about a business comes from?
7. What five things should you familiarize yourself with before going to your appointment?
8. Why should you categorize your survey questions?
9. What is the benefit of categorizing your survey questions?

10. What are some of the ways you can prepare for successful meetings?
11. Why is it important to make sure that project information is properly distributed?
12. Why may communication skills be more important than technical skills to a project manager?
13. Why should managing expectations be a concern for you?
14. What can happen if you do not monitor and control the project work?
15. What is the difference between monitoring a project and controlling a project? Why is it important that both of these are done?
16. Why should you update the people on the list of people that you need to talk to about the changes that are being made and their impacts?
17. What is included as a part of monitoring and controlling risks?
18. Why should you monitor and control risks in a project?

Debrief Questions

1. What are the key learning points?
2. What information was new to you?
3. What concepts will you apply in the future? When?
4. What challenges might limit your ability to apply the concepts?
5. What needs to be in place to overcome these challenges?
6. Who would you recommend these concepts to and why?

Activity

The following activity may be completed individually or in a small group to assess your comprehension.

1. Answer the discussion questions.
2. Answer the debrief questions.

CHAPTER 4

CELEBRATE

Later that evening, the celebrations start at an exclusive restaurant on Paradise Island. If anyone had any idea how much this evening cost, they would surely have opted for the Fish Fry. Oh well, this is a special occasion.

"Here's to success and a good night sleep." Mrs. Davis lifts her glass in a toast to John. "And to your continued success in applying project management skills to every aspect of your life."

Freddie, John's mother, brothers, and sister are all there. They raise their glasses in toasting John. "May you get an A grade on your coursework and become a coursework tutor."

"The world's a safer place," Freddie adds.

"You jokers!" John says, grinning broadly; his spirits are lifted high.

John's family takes him on a well-deserved holiday in South Florida. The coursework project is over. By all accounts, this experience is a success—but not without a mental and physical toll.

Who cares? John restores the relationships in his family. He is developing, focusing, and doing well in school. He feels a sense of purpose, and he is overjoyed!

Key Points to Remember

- When you close a project or phase, you finalize all activities to formally complete the project.

Applying to the Next Project

Debrief Questions

1.   What are the key learning points?
2.   What information was new to you?
3.   What concepts will you apply in the future? When?
4.   What challenges might limit your ability to apply the concepts?
5.   What needs to be in place to overcome these challenges?
6.   Who would you recommend these concepts to and why?

Activity

The following activity may be completed individually or in a small group to assess your comprehension.

1.   Answer the debrief questions.

Summary

John begins his journey toward coursework completion in somewhat of a vacuum. While he realizes early that his networking and relationship-building skills are underdeveloped, he soon accepts that completing his coursework project is more about people than processes. Beginning with his first meeting with Freddie—and throughout the course of the project—he is introduced to many experiences. From his coaching sessions with Mrs. Davis and building a relationship with his father, the processes for completing his coursework come alive. John's socialization early in the project is a turning point in his development and a key takeaway to use as a best practice when completing your coursework project.

With no prior experience, John recognizes his vulnerability and uses this to help him to develop skills in managing processes, people, and personalities.

John's journey exposes us to practical, easy-to-use, and easy-to-understand tools and techniques that empower him to reduce feelings of anxiety and manage people and processes. *Project Management Skills for Coursework* provides you with the expertise that you need to meet the requirements outlined in the Ministry of Education National Examinations Coursework Guide.

About the Author

Dorcas M. T. Cox is instructional designer and director of project services for Project Management Solutions Limited, a successful project management training and consultancy company. Project Management Solutions Limited offers a range of services while identifying and responding to your specific requirement. Project Management Solutions Limited offers

- standard and customized project management courses (including project essentials,
- project intermediate, and PMI certification); project management speakers bureau;
- on-site or off-site delivery of project management services;
- project team meeting facilitation; and project team coaching.

The author has more than eighteen years of instructional design and project management expertise to earn Project Management Solutions Limited the Registered Educational Provider designation from the Project Management Institute (REP #3627).

Project Management Institute's Registered Education Providers (REPs) are organizations approved by the Project Management Institute to offer project management training.

Dorcas has worked in government agencies as well as having designed instructional material for a multinational corporation that is used in English and Spanish throughout Central America and the Caribbean. She has facilitated training sessions in Canada and throughout the Bahamas and Caribbean, including Trinidad, Barbados, Belize, and St. Lucia. She continues to work as an adjunct instructor for academic institutions.

Dorcas has studied, lived, and worked in North America and Canada. She earned her Project Management Professional distinction from the Project Management Institute and lives in the Bahamas with her son. She can be reached via e-mail at dorcas.cox@gmail.com. You can also learn more about the products and services offered by Project Management Solutions Limited by visiting www.projectmanagementsolutionsltd.com

RESOURCES

Heldman, K. *PMP Project Management Professional Exam Study Guide*, 4th ed. Hoboken, NJ: Wiley Publishing, Inc., 2007.

The Ministry of Education National Examinations. Bahamas General Certificate of Secondary Educations (BGCSE) Coursework Guide. 2010.

Project Management Institute. *A Guide to the Project Management Body of Knowledge (PMBOK® Guide)*, 5th ed. Project Management Institute, 2013.

www.ingramcontent.com/pod-product-compliance
Lightning Source LLC
Chambersburg PA
CBHW030913180526
45163CB00004B/1813